THE ART OF

Smoke Cooking

COOKBOOK

Simple Recipes become Gourmet Delights
with the Art of Smoke Cooking

MILLY MCDONALD

The Art of Smoke Cooking Cookbook
By Milly McDonald

Photography: M.J. Cárdenas

Photo Art Direction: Milly McDonald

Food Styling: Lee Stanyer

Additional Food Styling: Cliff Ellman and Kat Hughes

Prop Procurement: Marie Cleavenger, Craig Schumacher, Philip Kirk and Cliff Ellman

Copy Editing: Lynn Clare

Book Design: Milly McDonald

Cover Design: Milly McDonald and Mike Story

Title Design: Mike Story

Layout Design: Milly McDonald and David Griffiths

Type Selection & Graphic Production: David Griffiths

Recipe Testing Assistant: Cheryl Tubbs

Special thanks to my mother, Shirley Hall, for teaching me to cook.

ACKNOWLEDGEMENTS
The author would like to thank the following people and organizations for their generous assistance and support in producing this book:
Thomas O'Higgins, Sandy Peterson and Sarah Esterling of Williams-Sonoma for believing in the concept from the beginning; my husband, Bill McDonald, for critiquing and enjoying my recipes; The Brinkmann Corporation for their wonderful smoker products.

Published by The Brinkmann Corporation
Printed in the United States of America

Contents

Introduction

Smoke cooking is an ancient culinary art. Early man discovered that aromatic wood smoke added flavor and naturally preserved foods. Throughout history, cultures around the world have applied the technique of smoke cooking to a wide variety of foods and recipes. Over the years, smoke cooking in the United States has become associated with holiday turkeys, hams and barbecue style briskets, ribs and chicken. These traditional smoked foods are still among my favorites and many are featured in this cookbook. However, *The Art of Smoke Cooking Cookbook* is dedicated to expanding the technique of smoke cooking to a much wider variety of foods and recipes.

Explore the pages of this cookbook and join a growing number of gourmet chefs and cooking enthusiasts who have rediscovered the art of smoke cooking. A culinary art that uses the smoking process to add flavor to foods that are then combined with other ingredients to create exciting new flavor combinations. Simple recipes become gourmet delights—pizza topped with smoked chicken, spaghetti with smoked meatballs, chicken fried steak made with smoked beef steak, chili con carne with smoked beef tenderloin, enchilada sauce made with smoked peppers, peach pie using smoked peaches. Simple and traditional recipes, all using smoked ingredients to add a unique flavor. After trying some of the recipes in this book, experiment with some of your own favorite recipes by smoking one or more of the ingredients.

And for today's health conscious gourmet, smoke cooking adds flavor without adding fat, calories or sodium. It's my favorite way to cook when I'm watching my weight. This slow, steamy, smoke-filled cooking process adds a delicious flavor to foods as it tenderizes. It's a wonderful way to cook extra lean cuts of beef, pork, skinless poultry, fish and vegetables. You will be amazed how delicious and succulent lean meats can be with smoke cooking. No more dry tasteless chicken breasts, no more bland steamed vegetables.

The following pages will review a wide variety of smoke cooking equipment, accessories, charcoal, aromatic smoking woods and steam marinades. Instructions for hot smoking and cold smoking, the two primary methods of smoke cooking, are described so that even the novice cook can easily master these techniques. You will learn how to use aromatic smoking woods and steam marinades as flavoring agents, just as you would herbs and spices. And best of all, forty delicious recipes illustrate how easy it is to cook like a master chef when you use the culinary art of smoke cooking. Smoke cooking is one of the best ways to add flavor to foods and it's so easy. Have fun, and *Bon Appétit.*

Smoke Cooking Equipment

Getting Started

All you need to get started is a well made outdoor smoker. I've been cooking on smokers for years and personally prefer Brinkmann to the other brands I've tried. I tested all the recipes in this cookbook on Brinkmann smokers and used many of their wonderful accessories. Brinkmann is the oldest manufacturer of outdoor smokers and offers the widest selection of smokers and accessories. Brinkmann sells under the brand names *Brinkmann, Smoke 'N Grill, Smoke 'N Pit, Cook 'N Cajun* and *Mr. Meat Smoker*. These smokers are available in fine gourmet catalogs, specialty stores, and grill departments of most major retail stores. To find out where to buy smokers in your area, call Brinkmann's toll-free number (1-800-HOT-5252).

Vertical Smokers

There are two types of outdoor smokers – vertical and horizontal. The most commonly used smokers are vertical smokers. They are more compact and less expensive than horizontal models. We'll discuss the virtues of horizontal smokers in a later section. Most vertical smokers are made of cold rolled steel and painted with a high quality powder-coated paint. Some manufacturers also offer stainless steel models. A typical vertical smoker has a cylindrical body approximately 16 inches in diameter and 30 to 42 inches in height, depending on the model. A domed lid sits on top of the body. The heat source – charcoal, electricity or gas – is located at the bottom or base of the smoker body. Aromatic flavoring woods or herbs are placed on or near the heat source to produce smoke. Directly above the heat source is a pan containing water or flavored marinade which becomes steam as the liquid heats. This steam marinade combines with the smoke to naturally tenderize and flavor the food. The food rests on grills positioned above the water pan. Most smokers have two grills – one positioned above the other – each capable of holding about 25 pounds of food. A large turkey and a large roast can easily be smoked at the same time. The domed lid is positioned on top of the smoker body to contain most of the heat, smoke and steam. The aromatic smoke and steam baste the food while the indirect heat slowly cooks the food. The result is the most delicious, succulent foods you'll ever taste, with no added fat or calories.

Charcoal Smokers

The charcoal smoker is the original and most commonly used vertical smoker. A charcoal pan at the bottom or base of the smoker holds 10 to 15 pounds of charcoal. Aromatic wood chunks or herbs are placed on the charcoal to produce aromatic smoke. As in all vertical smokers, a water pan is positioned above the heat source. Two grills above the water pan hold food, and a domed lid sits atop the smoker body to contain the heat, smoke and steam. A good charcoal smoker will have a temperature gauge in the domed lid so that the cook can see when the cooking temperature is ideal and when the charcoal's heating energy is declining.

The charcoal smoker's widespread popularity is primarily due to its low cost relative to electric and gas smokers and its portability. A charcoal smoker is easy to take along to a campsite, lake house or cookout location. Charcoal smokers are relatively lightweight and require no electrical outlets or bulky propane gas tanks. And because many consumers are familiar with charcoal grilling, they are more comfortable with a charcoal smoker. But don't mistakenly select a charcoal smoker over an electric or gas model because you believe that foods cooked in a charcoal smoker taste better than foods cooked in electric or gas smokers. I have found that the heat source does not affect the flavor of smoked foods. Foods cooked in a smoker get their flavor from the aromatic wood smoke and the steam marinade, not from the heat source itself.

The main disadvantage of a charcoal smoker as compared to an electric or gas smoker is that charcoal has a limited burn time and the heat it produces is not constant. As charcoal burns, it gradually loses heat and the temperature inside the smoker drops. For this reason, smoke cooking in a charcoal smoker will require a longer cooking time than in an electric or gas smoker and may require adding more charcoal during the cooking process. If you like to lift the domed lid to check your food, consider buying an electric or gas smoker. Frequent removal of the lid will result in a substantial loss of heat in a charcoal smoker. Cold temperatures and high winds will also affect the temperature inside a charcoal smoker more than in an electric or gas smoker. Smoked foods are great in the fall and winter as well as in the spring and summer, so consider an electric or gas model if you plan to use your smoker year round.

However, if you are looking for an inexpensive way to get started with smoke cooking, a charcoal smoker is your best bet. Most retail stores carry Brinkmann's charcoal smokers at very affordable prices.

Charcoal Smoker Cooking Tips:

Never use a self-starting charcoal that contains starting agents impregnated in the charcoal. This type of charcoal will burn too quickly to fully cook your food and may impart an undesirable flavor. Use a high quality standard charcoal or, even better, an all hardwood charcoal such as Brinkmann's *Smoker's Blend*. Every bag of *Smoker's Blend* contains several aromatic smoking wood briquets which are made of compressed hickory or mesquite wood shavings. These briquets produce aromatic smoke and eliminate the need for wood chunks.

Because a pan full of charcoal produces a limited supply of heat, you will need to preserve as much heat inside the cooker as possible. Heat will be lost by removing the lid to check your food, so resist this temptation as much as possible. When cooking for long periods, you may need to add more charcoal briquets during the cooking process.

Excessive wind will also make the charcoal burn faster, so try to place your smoker where wind is minimized. Remember, never use a smoker indoors; fumes from the charcoal and wood are toxic. Always follow smoker manufacturer's operating instructions and safety warnings.

Electric Smokers

In recent years, vertical electric smokers have gained a strong following among smoke cooking enthusiasts due to their ease of use, versatility and reliability. Unlike the charcoal smoker, the electric smoker provides a constant and unlimited heat source through an electric element at the bottom or base of the smoker. Many electric smokers do not come equipped with a temperature gauge because the cooking temperature of an electric smoker will usually be ideal and a temperature gauge is rarely needed. Most electric smokers provide a bed of lava rocks or a metal plate on which the electric element rests. Aromatic wood chunks or herbs are placed on the lava rocks or in a metal pan on top of the electric element. Like all vertical smokers, a pan containing water or flavored marinade is positioned above the heat source. Two grills above the water pan hold food, and a domed lid sits atop the smoker body to contain the heat, smoke and steam.

The primary advantage of an electric smoker is its constant and unlimited heat source. All you need is a suitable outdoor electrical outlet – no hassling with charcoal or charcoal starters. Although the initial cost of an electric smoker is usually greater than a charcoal smoker, the cost of charcoal and lighter fluid can really add up with regular use. An electric smoker is easy to set up, and for those of us who like to smoke cook frequently that's a real advantage. If you prefer to lift the domed lid to check your food frequently, the electric smoker is more reliable. Unlike the charcoal smoker, the temperature inside the electric smoker will build up again quickly after the lid is replaced. Cooking times are shorter with an electric smoker, and you can cook large amounts of food at one time without worrying about a diminishing fuel supply. High winds and cold temperatures also have less effect on an electric smoker. The smoke cooking process may take a little longer when it's cold and windy, but the constant heat source will always get the job done.

Another important advantage of an electric smoker is its versatility. All smokers can be used to water smoke, dry smoke, steam/poach, bake and cold smoke, but I find the electric smoker the easiest to use for all these methods. To use as a dry smoker, simply eliminate the water pan, use aromatic wood chunks and plug the smoker into an electrical outlet. To use as a steamer/poacher, place your food on the grill above the water pan filled with water or flavored marinade, eliminate the wood chunks and plug in the smoker. To bake in an electric smoker, simply eliminate the water pan and the wood chunks. For cold smoking, eliminate the water pan and unplug the smoker after the wood chunks have started smoking. The food inside the smoker will absorb the smoke flavor without cooking. Cold smoking is used to smoke meats and vegetables that require cooking after smoking, such as steak that will be chicken fried.

Electric Smoker Cooking Tips:

If you are accustomed to cooking with a charcoal smoker, you may be surprised how much faster an electric smoker cooks. I recommend that you check the doneness of your food a little earlier in the cooking process than you might expect to avoid overcooking. It's always better to undercook than overcook. With a constant heat source, food can always be returned to the smoker for additional cooking, but overcooking cannot be undone.

A quality meat thermometer is the best way to test the doneness of your meats. Of course, another method of testing the doneness of meat is to cut into the thickest portion. Remember, a large cut of meat will continue to cook a little after it has been removed from the smoker due to the heat contained inside the meat itself.

On especially cold or windy days, you may have to allow extra cooking time. Longer cooking times may require adding more liquid to the water pan. Always follow smoker manufacturer's operating instructions and safety warnings.

Gas Smokers

The gas smoker is considered by some to be the king of vertical smokers. Like the electric smoker, the gas smoker has a constant heat source in the form of a propane gas burner at the base of the smoker body. Most gas smokers also have an adjustable burner which permits variable cooking temperatures. The higher temperature setting can be a real advantage when cooking in cold temperatures or in windy conditions. A typical gas smoker should be set up with a 20-pound propane gas storage tank. The tank is connected by a hose and regulator to a gas burner which rests on a bed of lava rocks in the base of the smoker. Aromatic wood chunks or herbs are placed on the lava rocks to produce smoke, and a water pan is positioned above the heat source. Two grills above the water pan hold food, and a domed lid sits atop the smoker body to contain the heat, smoke and steam.

Not only does the gas smoker provide an adjustable and constant heat source, it has the additional advantage of portability because it does not depend on an electrical outlet. A gas smoker is a great choice for out-of-the-way locations, campsites and cookouts. If you prefer a constant heat source and an electrical outlet is not available, then the gas smoker is the right model for you. Again, for those in cold climates who like to cook in the fall and winter months, the variable temperature control is a real plus. If you are in the habit of frequently removing the domed lid to check on your food, the gas smoker is a good choice because the heat inside will build up again rapidly after the lid is replaced. Of course, the gas smoker is the most expensive of the three vertical smokers.

I enjoy cooking on the gas smoker, but the electric smoker is still my favorite. I don't like to spend time assembling things and the electric smoker is much easier to assemble than the gas smoker. I have an outdoor plug conveniently located at my home and I like the idea of simply plugging in the smoker and never having to worry about refilling the propane tank. I like to smoke cook often, and the electric model is the easiest for me to set up and manage by myself.

The gas smoker is gaining in popularity due to its ease of use and economical fuel. The cost per use of a gas smoker is much less than that of a charcoal smoker. Even an electric smoker costs more to use than a gas smoker. Another popular feature of the gas smoker is its ability to easily convert to a gas grill. Charcoal, electric and gas smokers can all be used as a barbecue grill; however, the gas model is the best choice for grilling because the variable heat control, waist-level height and lava rocks make it perform like a conventional gas grill.

Gas Smoker Cooking Tips:

Like the electric, the gas smoker cooks faster than charcoal and you must be careful not to overcook your foods. Also, like the electric, you may need to add more liquid to the water pan when smoke cooking over a long period of time. Because a gas smoker cooks a little hotter, the wood chunks may burn too fast. The solution is simple: after soaking the wood chunks in water, wrap them in aluminum foil and punch holes in the foil to allow smoke to be released. The aluminum foil slows the burning process and the wood chunks smoke over a longer period of time. Always follow smoker manufacturer's operating instructions and safety warnings.

15

Horizontal Smokers

The horizontal smoker is the ideal smoker for the outdoor chef who wants to cook large quantities of food at one time. The horizontal design provides a large cooking surface on one easily accessible level. The heat source is contained in a separate fire chamber affixed to the side of a cooking chamber. Both fire and cooking chambers are typically 16-inch wide cylinders with the cooking chamber measuring at least twice as long as the fire chamber. A wood or charcoal fire is built inside the fire chamber, and a vented smokestack (chimney) draws the heat and smoke through the cooking chamber. Large quantities of food rest on a grill surface inside the cooking chamber where the food absorbs the indirect heat and smoke. The cooking temperature can be adjusted up or down by adjusting air vents and increasing or reducing the air flow through the fire chamber. For those who prefer a moist smoke cooking environment, a water pan can be placed inside the cooking chamber next to the fire chamber. The fire chamber can also be used as a standard barbecue grill by placing a grill directly above the coals.

The primary advantage of a horizontal smoker is its large cooking capacity on a single level. To get the same capacity in a standard vertical model would require a smoker so tall that a ladder would be needed to reach the food. The horizontal design provides a large grill surface at one accessible height.

Another advantage of the horizontal smoker is the fire chamber's ability to house an all wood burning fire. For those who prefer a more intense smoke flavor, an all wood fire provides the greatest amount of smoke and smoke flavor.

Gourmet cooks will also appreciate how easy it is to

slow smoke and cold smoke foods in a large horizontal smoker. Cold smoking utilizes smoke with very little or no heat. A horizontal smoker is perfect for this process because of the distance between the fire and the far end of the cooking chamber. One or two wood chunks can be lit in the fire chamber and the food placed in the opposite end of the smoker where it absorbs minimum heat. The smoke flavor will be absorbed without cooking the food. Read more about cold smoking in a later section entitled "The Basics of Smoke Cooking."

There are a few disadvantages to a large horizontal smoker, one of which is expense. A large horizontal smoker costs much more than any of the standard vertical smokers. And because of its size and weight, the horizontal smoker is not as portable as its smaller vertical counterparts. As with any charcoal or wood burning smoker, the heat source is not constant which can lead to a loss of heat. This can be a problem in cold and windy weather or if you open the lid often to check your food. You may have to add more fuel to the fire chamber during the smoke cooking process to maintain the proper temperature. But if you want to smoke cook a large quantity of food at one time, the horizontal smoker is the best choice.

Horizontal Smoker Cooking Tips:

When smoke cooking large quantities of food, be careful to adjust the airflow vents so that the fire will not cook too hot and burn out too soon. Never close the airflow vents completely unless you want to extinguish your fire. You can monitor your cooking temperature with a temperature gauge inserted in the lid of the smoker. If a temperature gauge is not included with the model you purchase, buy one where you bought your smoker or order one direct from the manufacturer. When cooking large cuts of meat such as turkeys, hams and large roasts, place the food at the far end of the cooking chamber away from the fire. This will allow the food to smoke cook more slowly over a longer period of time. If the temperature begins to decline before you have finished the smoke cooking process, add more fuel until the temperature rises to the desired level.

Smoke Cooking Accessories

A wide variety of smoker accessories is available to make the smoke cooking process easier and more versatile. Brinkmann offers the widest variety of smoker accessories under the *Smokeshop* brand name. These accessories can be found wherever Brinkmann smokers are sold or can be ordered directly from Brinkmann by calling toll free 1-800-HOT-5252. I have described the accessories I use most frequently and find to be the most useful.

Smoker Basket. The smoker basket is the most essential of all smoke cooking accessories. I use it every time I cook with a smoker.

The basket is constructed of nickel-plated steel wire in a basket weave pattern. The primary purpose of the smoker basket is to contain food that might otherwise fall through the grill while allowing the smoke, steam and heat to pass through. The secondary purpose of the smoker basket is to provide a convenient method for lifting food in and out of the smoker. The basket is approximately two inches deep and 15 inches in diameter and rests on top of the wire grill. It has two handles on either side for lifting in and out of the smoker. The size of the openings in the basket weave prevents food from falling through while still allowing the smoke, steam and heat to flow through the basket and into the food. I use it for smoking fish, shellfish, meatloaf, pâté, pizza, vegetables, fruit and appetizers. Because it's so easy to take food in and out of the smoker when it's inside the smoker basket, I also use it for large items like turkey, ham and tenderloin.

Meat Thermometer. When smoking large cuts of meat, I always use a meat thermometer to test for doneness. Inserting a meat thermometer into the thickest portion of the meat is the best way to determine if it is cooked to the desired doneness. Without a meat thermometer, you should cut into the thickest part of the meat to test for doneness. Since I don't like cutting into the beautiful smoked meats I prepare, I always use a meat thermometer. You can never correct an overcooked cut of meat, so take the guesswork out and buy a good meat thermometer.

Horizontal Smoker Temperature Gauge. If you purchase a large horizontal smoker without a temperature gauge, you will need to purchase a temperature gauge to be inserted in the smoker lid. A gauge can be purchased either from the retail store or ordered directly from

the manufacturer. Remember, the cooking temperature of a wood/charcoal burning horizontal smoker is regulated by adjusting the airflow vents and by adding more wood and charcoal. Even a slight adjustment of the airflow vents can affect the temperature, and the best way to monitor this is a reliable temperature gauge. When I use the horizontal smoker, I am usually cooking large quantities of food at a low constant heat over a long period of time. A temperature gauge shows me when I need to adjust the airflow or add fuel to maintain the temperature.

Rib-Rack Holder. The rib-rack holder is terrific for smoke cooking several racks of ribs, corn on the cob and baked potatoes at one time. The rib-rack holder is designed to contain several racks of ribs in a vertical position to conserve space and to allow the smoke and steam to penetrate the ribs evenly. Vertical spikes at the corners can be used to hold corn on the cob, potatoes, mushrooms and onions. The rib-rack holder is constructed of nickel-plated wire and sits directly on top of the grill. It can also be placed in the smoker basket for easy lifting in and out of the smoker. I always use the rib-rack holder when I smoke ribs because

I can cook four times as many ribs. Brinkmann's vertical smokers can hold up to two rib-rack holders and their horizontal smoker can hold up to six rib-rack holders.

Smoke Cooking Spices. When you have the time, you should experiment with your own blend of herbs and spices. But when you're in a hurry, Brinkmann's *Smoke 'N Spice* blends are your best bet. Brinkmann's pre-packaged blends of herbs and spices have been specially formulated to enhance the flavor of smoked foods. Brinkmann's *Smoke 'N Spice* brand red meat and white meat blends are both made without MSG. One is formulated to work best with red meats and the other works best with white meats and vegetables. I use these spices often when smoke cooking because I love the flavor and it saves me the time of preparing my own blend.

Charcoal, Aromatic Woods and Steam Marinades

Charcoal

Never use a self-starting charcoal that contains starting agents impregnated in the charcoal. This type of charcoal will burn too quickly to fully cook your food and may impart an undesirable flavor. Use a high quality standard charcoal or, even better, an all hardwood charcoal such as Brinkmann's *Smoker's Blend*. This all hardwood charcoal is made from hickory wood with no added petroleum products – just pure charcoal derived from hickory hardwood. Hardwood charcoal is long burning and burns cleaner than charcoals containing high levels of coal and petroleum additives. And every 10-pound bag of *Smoker's Blend* charcoal contains several briquets formed from hickory or mesquite wood shavings. These briquets take the place of wood chunks, so all you need is a bag of *Smoker's Blend* and you're ready to smoke. And there's no better charcoal to use for grilling. *Smoker's Blend* charcoal is usually available where quality smokers are sold. To find out where to buy *Smoker's Blend* charcoal in your area or to order direct, call Brinkmann's toll-free number 1-800-HOT-5252.

Aromatic Smoking Woods

Think of aromatic smoking woods as you would herbs or spices. The flavor of food can be altered by using aromatic wood smoke, and different types of wood impart distinctly different flavors. Combining a particular aromatic wood with a particular food is an important aspect of the art of smoke cooking. For example, pecan smoked chicken and mesquite smoked chicken are both delicious but the flavors are distinctly

different. Rosemary smoked salmon and alder smoked salmon each have a unique flavor, delicious but different. Part of the fun of smoke cooking is experimenting with a variety of aromatic woods. Hardwoods, especially fruit and nut tree woods, are the most desirable for aromatic smoking. Coniferous woods such as pine and cedar contain high levels of tar and should never be used. My favorite aromatic smoking woods are hickory, mesquite, pecan, oak, alder, maple, walnut, olive, apple, peach and grapevine. Dried stalks of rosemary, basil, sage, thyme and oregano also impart a delicious flavor to foods when used for aromatic smoking. Experimenting with different woods and herbs can result in delightful flavor combinations. The recipes in this book are intended to be a tried and true guide, but don't be afraid to experiment with various aromatic woods.

Small wood chips and flakes do not work well for smoke cooking because they burn too quickly and do not release smoke over a long period of time. Larger wood chunks or blocks are the best form of wood to use for smoking. To slow down the burning process, soak wood chunks in water for an hour. For even slower smoking, wrap wood chunks in foil and poke holes in the foil to allow the release of smoke. The objective is to get a moderate amount of smoke over a longer period of time. A good rule of thumb is to use three to four wood chunks per smoking. If you desire an intense smoke flavor, add more wood chunks as you see the smoke from the original wood diminish. Most foods are best when not oversmoked, so be careful.

Steam Marinades

Like aromatic woods, think of the liquid you use in the water pan as a flavoring agent. Not only does the steam from the liquid add flavor, it also tenderizes food. A turkey steamed in cranberry juice will have an entirely different flavor than a turkey steamed in orange juice. Both are delicious, but the tastes are distinctly different. Combine aromatic smoke with steam marinade and the result is a unique culinary delight. Hickory smoked turkey steamed in orange juice is far more delicious than a plain baked turkey. I encourage you to experiment with a variety of steam marinades to familiarize yourself with the various flavors they impart. The most popular steam marinades are red wines, white wines, fruit juices of all types, beers, liquors, liqueurs and traditional marinades. You will discover a world of flavors to enhance the taste of your food without adding fat, calories or sodium. And you won't miss the fat because the steaming process adds succulence to vegetables and lean cuts of meats, poultry and fish.

The Basics of Smoke Cooking

Early man discovered aromatic wood smoke made foods taste better and preserved them naturally. Throughout history, cultures around the world have applied the technique of smoke cooking to a wide variety of foods and recipes. Over the years, traditional smoke cooking in the United States has become primarily associated with holiday turkeys, hams and barbecue style briskets, ribs and chicken. These traditional smoked foods are still among my favorites and many are featured in this cookbook, but the art of smoke cooking can be applied to a much wider variety of foods and recipes. Explore the pages of this cookbook and join a growing number of gourmet chefs and cooking enthusiasts who have rediscovered the art of smoke cooking. A culinary art that uses the smoking process to add flavor to foods that are then combined with other ingredients to create exciting new recipes. Traditional shrimp scampi becomes smoked shrimp scampi, traditional fried chicken becomes smoked fried chicken, traditional tomato soup becomes smoked tomato soup.

Even the novice cook can master the art of smoke cooking by applying the following basics.

Creative Use of Smoked Ingredients

You can transform simple recipes into gourmet delights by creatively using smoked ingredients. Pizza topped with smoked mushrooms, spaghetti with smoked meatballs, chicken fried steak made with smoked steak, tomato soup using smoked tomatoes, chili con carne with smoked beef tenderloin, enchilada sauce made with smoked tomatoes and peppers. Simple and traditional recipes, all using smoked ingredients to add flavor and distinction. The possibilities are endless: pasta dishes made with smoked meat, poultry, seafood or vegetables; sauces made from smoked peppers or tomatoes; soups made from smoked vegetables or smoked chicken stock; dessert toppings and pies made with smoked fruits; dips and spreads made with smoked seafood or vegetables; casseroles made with smoked meats; omelets made with smoked cheese, meat or vegetables. After trying a few of the recipes in this book, experiment with some of your own favorites by smoking one or more of the ingredients. You'll be amazed how easy it is to create your own signature dishes with smoke cooking. And for today's health conscious gourmet, smoke cooking adds flavor without adding fat, calories or sodium.

Aromatic Woods and Steam Marinades as Flavoring Agents

Think of aromatic woods and steam marinades as flavoring agents, just as you would herbs and spices. As the wood and liquid marinade vaporize inside the smoker, this moist smoke penetrates the food and leaves its delicious flavors behind. Various aromatic woods and steam marinades produce a variety of flavors, just as different herbs and spices add different flavors. The flavors produced by hickory wood smoke are different from those produced by alder wood smoke.

22

Red wine steam marinade imparts an entirely different flavor than orange juice steam marinade. After trying some of the recipes in this book, don't be afraid to experiment with your own combinations of aromatic woods and steam marinades. Experimenting is the best way to get to know the various flavors and a sure way of creating some delicious and unique recipes of your own.

Hot Smoking Method

Hot smoking is the most commonly used method of smoking and should be used whenever the recipe calls for the smoked food to be fully cooked. Because the hot smoking method combines heat and smoke, it cooks and smokes food at the same time. Hot smoking is the only method that turns liquid marinade into steam. Typical examples of hot smoked foods are smoked ribs, smoked turkey and smoked meatloaf. Hot smoked foods usually require no additional cooking after being removed from the smoker. Of course, if a lighter smoked flavor is preferred, the hot smoking method can be used to partially cook the food in the smoker before finishing the cooking process using the range top or oven.

When hot smoking, follow the smoker manufacturer's guidelines for cooking times, but remember they are only meant to be guidelines. There are too many variables in the smoke cooking process to precisely pinpoint cooking times. Remember, it is better to undercook than to overcook. It's easy to return the food to the smoker for additional cooking but impossible to undo overcooking. Use a meat thermometer or test your foods by cutting into the center.

Cold Smoking Method

The cold smoking method is used when the recipe calls for the food to be flavored with smoke, but not cooked. You should use the cold smoking method when the recipe calls for a raw smoked ingredient or when the recipe requires additional cooking of the smoked ingredient after removing it from the smoker. Hickory Smoked Veal Parmesan calls for the raw veal to be cold smoked for thirty minutes to give it a rich smoke flavor. Then, the mostly raw, cold smoked veal is breaded and sautéed in oil before oven baking with red sauce and cheese for 30 minutes.

Cold smoking is accomplished by slowly burning one or two wood chunks with as little heat as possible. Because there is very little heat produced, steam marinades are not used with this method. In a charcoal smoker, wood chunks are placed on top of no more than two to three burning charcoal briquets. When the wood begins to smoke, the food is placed on the top grill where it will be exposed to smoke but very little heat. As discussed in an earlier section, the electric and gas smokers are the best models to use for cold smoking. As the lava rocks heat and the wood chunks begin to smoke, the electric or gas heat source should be turned off. Again, the food is placed on the top grill where it will be exposed to minimum heat.

Recipes

The following pages contain a selection of my favorite smoke cooking recipes. Most of them are remarkably simple to prepare — yet exceptional in taste, texture and presentation. I hope you enjoy these recipes and will experiment with your own smoke cooked creations. Remember that smoking times can vary, so use the times prescribed as a general guideline for your individual preference.

HICKORY SMOKED TURKEY, HONEY GLAZED AND STEAMED IN CITRUS MARINADE

*A*smoked turkey is much more flavorful and succulent than a roast turkey, and this particular recipe gets rave reviews at holiday dinners and special occasions. Glazing the turkey with honey gives it a golden color and using concentrated orange juice in the water pan steams the turkey with a delightful marinade. Smoking the giblets makes for a uniquely delicious giblet gravy. Fresh, uncooked ham can also be prepared using the following recipes. Hickory and oak are the best smoking woods for turkey and ham.

Ingredients:

A 10- to 12-lb turkey

1 cup honey

2 tablespoons each celery powder and garlic powder*

*May substitute 4 tablespoons Smoke 'N Spice white meat seasoning (see page 19)

4 16-oz cans orange juice concentrate (reserve $^1/_4$ cup concentrate; mix remainder with water to fill water pan)

6 hickory wood chunks, water soaked and wrapped in foil with holes to insure long smoking

Remove giblets and rinse turkey. Gently lift skin and rub turkey with a thick coating of honey mixed with $^1/_4$ cup orange juice concentrate, celery powder and garlic powder. Replace skin to its original position and rub a thick coating of honey and celery/garlic powder mixture all over surface of skin.

Place wood chunks on charcoal or lava rocks, and pour orange juice mixture into water pan. Place giblets and turkey in smoker basket (see page 18) with breast upright and set on lower level grill. Smoke cook for approximately 3 to 5 hours (electric/gas smoker) or 6 to 8 hours (charcoal smoker). Use a meat thermometer to test doneness.

Skim fat from liquid in water pan to make gravy. Add smoked giblets to gravy. Serves 10.

HICKORY SMOKED TURKEY, MOLASSES GLAZED AND STEAMED IN PINEAPPLE MARINADE

For a slightly sweet tasting smoked turkey, substitute molasses in place of honey and crushed pineapple in place of orange juice in the water pan. Another variation — use sweet cranberry sauce in place of honey and cranberry juice in place of orange juice concentrate in the water pan.

Smoking the Italian sausage gives it a rich smoky flavor that permeates the pasta sauce when sautéed with olive oil, garlic and basil. Anyone who appreciates gourmet Italian cuisine will love this spicy dish.

Ingredients:

*4 oak wood chunks
(use hickory as substitute)*

*3 cups dry white wine for
water pan*

*1 1/2 lb spicy Italian sausage links,
cut into 1-inch pieces*

6 tablespoons extra virgin olive oil

4 cloves garlic, chopped

1/2 cup caper juice

1/2 cup dry white wine

1/4 cup water

3/4 cup chopped fresh basil

*1 1/2 lb bow tie pasta, cooked
al dente and drained*

1/4 cup capers

*1/2 cup freshly grated
Parmesan cheese*

Freshly ground pepper

Place wood chunks on charcoal or lava rocks, and pour wine into water pan. Distribute Italian sausage pieces evenly in smoker basket (see page 18) and set on lower level grill. Smoke cook for approximately 45 minutes to 1 hour (electric/gas smoker) or 1 to 1 1/2 hours (charcoal smoker).

In a large sauce pan heat olive oil over medium heat, add garlic and sauté for about 5 minutes, stirring constantly. Add caper juice, wine, water and smoked sausage. Bring to a gentle boil, reduce heat, cover and simmer for 15 to 20 minutes. Add basil and simmer for only 2 minutes more (basil loses its flavor if overcooked).

Add cooked pasta to sauce mixture, toss and heat until pasta is piping hot. Stir in capers just before removing from heat. Garnish with Parmesan cheese and fresh cracked pepper. The salt in the caper juice should be enough; season only after tasting. Serves 6.

OAK SMOKED PORK LOIN WITH PASTA IN SMOKY GARLIC SAUCE

For a less spicy dish, substitute medallions of smoked pork loin or strips of smoked pork chops in place of the Italian sausage. If smoking a whole tenderloin, allow a little extra cooking time and use a meat thermometer to test for doneness.

MESQUITE SMOKED CHICKEN CAESAR SALAD WITH SESAME PARMESAN DRESSING

*U*sing mesquite wood and beer as the steam marinade gives the chicken breasts a flavor that is undeniably Southwestern. The combination of smoked chicken breasts, toasted sesame seeds and Parmesan cheese make this Caesar salad a light meal with a delicious rich flavor.

Ingredients:

3 mesquite wood chunks

4 cups beer for water pan

4 skinless boneless chicken breasts

3 heads romaine lettuce

$^1/_4$ cup lightly toasted sesame seeds

$^1/_2$ cup extra virgin olive oil

$^1/_8$ cup white wine or balsamic vinegar

2 tablespoons Dijon mustard

$1^1/_2$ cups freshly grated Parmesan cheese

Salt and freshly ground pepper to taste

Place wood chunks on charcoal or lava rocks, and pour beer into water pan. Place chicken breasts in smoker basket (see page 18) and set on lower level grill. Smoke cook until done, approximately 30 minutes (electric/gas smoker) or 45 minutes (charcoal smoker).

Remove chicken breasts from smoker and cut into $^1/_4$- by 2-inch strips. Cover and set aside in refrigerator. Wash and drain lettuce, remove ends and chop into 2-inch pieces. Cover and set aside in refrigerator.

Evenly distribute sesame seeds on a baking pan or cookie sheet and toast in preheated oven at 350° F. for about 5 minutes or until golden brown. In a glass jar mix olive oil, vinegar, mustard, Parmesan cheese and sesame seeds. Stir until well blended, cover and refrigerate.

After all ingredients have been chilled for at least 30 minutes, toss smoked chicken strips, lettuce and dressing in a large serving bowl. Add salt and pepper to taste and toss again. Serve immediately while still well chilled. Serves 6.

MESQUITE SMOKED CHICKEN SPINACH SALAD WITH BACON PARMESAN DRESSING

For a delicious Southwestern style spinach salad, substitute fresh spinach in place of romaine and well cooked crumbled bacon in place of the sesame seeds.

PECAN SMOKED PEPPERED BEEF TENDERLOIN STEAMED IN RED WINE MARINADE

*T*his gourmet entrée is unbelievably easy to prepare and guaranteed to impress your guests every time you serve it. The pecan smoke gives the meat a rich reddish color and the taste is superb. A California Cabernet Sauvignon or a Merlot wine used as a steam marinade adds a robust flavor that is unique to this recipe.

Ingredients:

An 8- to 10-lb beef tenderloin, trimmed of fat

2 tablespoons garlic powder or Smoke 'N Spice red meat seasoning (see page 19)

1 tablespoon freshly ground pepper

4 pecan wood chunks (use hickory as substitute)

1 bottle (750 ml) Cabernet Sauvignon or Merlot red wine for water pan (reserve ¹/₂ cup for sauce)

Use an ice pick or long pronged fork to poke holes throughout the tenderloin so aromatic smoke and steam marinade can easily penetrate the meat. Rub the outside surface of the tenderloin with garlic powder and pepper.

Place wood chunks on charcoal or lava rocks, and pour wine into water pan. Place tenderloin in smoker basket (see page18) and set on lower level grill. Smoke cook for approximately $1\frac{1}{2}$ to 2 hours (electric/gas smoker) or $2\frac{1}{2}$ to 3 hours (charcoal smoker) for medium rare, longer if you prefer it to be more well done. If your guests have varying preferences of doneness, cut the tenderloin in half and cook the two sections for varying lengths of time. In my opinion, a tenderloin is best medium rare but should never be cooked beyond medium. Use a meat thermometer to test doneness.

Prepare a natural juice sauce by simmering $\frac{1}{2}$ cup red wine, $\frac{1}{2}$ cup water and $\frac{1}{2}$ cup chopped smoked tenderloin in a sauce pan for 15 minutes. Add salt and pepper to taste. Slice tenderloin and serve warm. Serves 10.

PECAN SMOKED PEPPERED PORK TENDERLOIN, MAPLE GLAZED AND STEAMED IN RED WINE MARINADE

For pork lovers, substitute pork tenderloin in place of beef. Also, drench pork tenderloin in maple syrup before rubbing it with garlic powder and pepper.

HICKORY SMOKED CHICKEN FRIED STEAK WITH SPICY CREAM GRAVY

*C*old smoking meats before frying, baking or sautéing adds a wonderful smoked flavor to traditionally prepared foods. This chicken fried steak recipe uses the best quality steaks that are cold smoked, then floured and fried. Even the cream gravy has a hint of smoky flavor from the fried steak drippings. These smoky steaks make delicious sandwiches, too.

Ingredients:

Chicken Fried Steaks:

3 hickory wood chunks

6 8-oz beef round steaks

4 cups buttermilk

2$\frac{1}{2}$ cups flour

2$\frac{1}{4}$ teaspoons garlic salt

1 teaspoon freshly ground pepper

Canola oil for frying

Cream Gravy:

10 tablespoons flour

7 cups milk

1 teaspoon Tabasco

1$\frac{1}{4}$ teaspoons freshly ground pepper

Place dry wood chunks on charcoal or lava rocks; do not use liquid in water pan. Pound or have butcher pound steaks to tenderize until about $\frac{1}{16}$- to $\frac{1}{8}$-inch thick. Place steaks in smoker basket (see page 18) and set on upper level grill. Cold smoke (see page 23) steaks for 30 minutes.

Place smoked steaks in a shallow casserole dish and pour in buttermilk. Cover and refrigerate for 12 to 16 hours. The buttermilk will further tenderize the steaks. Combine flour, garlic salt and pepper in a bowl and mix thoroughly. Remove steaks from buttermilk and coat with flour mixture.

Pour 1 inch of canola oil into a large frying skillet and heat over medium heat until lightly smoking. Fry steaks about 1$\frac{1}{2}$ to 2 minutes per side until golden brown. Remove steaks, drain on paper towels and keep warm.

To make gravy, keep 8 tablespoons of oil with drippings in the frying pan. Over medium heat, blend flour and oil with a whisk and cook until golden brown, whisking continuously. Gradually pour in milk as you whisk until gravy is blended to a creamy consistency. Blend in Tabasco, pepper and salt to taste. Serve gravy piping hot over steaks and mashed potatoes. Serves 6.

HICKORY SMOKED VEAL PARMESAN BAKED IN RED SAUCE WITH CHEESE

For a new twist on a traditional Italian dish, cold smoke and fry thinly sliced and pounded veal steaks as in the above recipe. Place fried steaks in casserole dish and cover with your favorite marinara sauce. Top with a thick layer of mozzarella and Parmesan cheese. Cover and bake in a preheated oven at 350° F. for 20 to 30 minutes until bubbly hot.

MESQUITE SMOKED CHICKEN, PEPPER & ONION PIZZA WITH TWO CHEESES

This fabulous pizza recipe uses smoked toppings – chicken, onions and peppers. The pizza is then baked with a special barbecue and fresh tomato sauce, and garnished with pine nuts. Create your own signature pizzas by smoking some of your favorite toppings.

Ingredients:

3 mesquite wood chunks

3 cups dry white wine for water pan

3 skinless boneless chicken breasts

1½ cups barbecue sauce

1 red sweet onion, thinly sliced

1 bell pepper, thinly sliced

Pizza dough mix

3 cloves garlic, minced

2 cups chopped Roma tomatoes

½ cup extra virgin olive oil

¼ cup dried oregano

3 cups shredded mozzarella cheese

1 cup freshly grated Parmesan cheese

2 tablespoons pine nuts

Place wood chunks on charcoal or lava rocks, and pour wine into water pan. Slice chicken breasts into ¼- by 2-inch strips. Coat chicken pieces with barbecue sauce; set remaining sauce aside. Place chicken strips, sliced onion and pepper in smoker basket (see page 18) and set on lower level grill. Smoke cook until chicken is done, approximately 30 minutes (electric/gas smoker) or 45 minutes (charcoal smoker). Remove chicken and vegetables from smoker, cover and set aside.

Preheat oven to 425° F. Prepare pizza dough according to package directions and spread on a 14-inch round baking sheet. In a sauce pan, sauté garlic in ¼ cup olive oil for 5 minutes. Add barbecue sauce, tomatoes and oregano. Bring to a gentle boil, reduce to medium heat and simmer for about 20 to 30 minutes until sauce is thickened.

Brush pizza dough all over with olive oil. Cover dough with mozzarella and Parmesan cheese, leaving a ½-inch border around the edges. Cover cheese with sauce mixture and arrange smoked chicken, onions and peppers on top. Drizzle evenly with remaining olive oil and sprinkle with pine nuts. Bake in preheated oven at 425° F. for 20 minutes. Slice and serve. Serves 4.

MESQUITE SMOKED SAUSAGE, PEPPER & ONION PIZZA WITH TWO CHEESES

For a more traditional style pizza, substitute your favorite prepared pizza sauce in place of the barbecue sauce mixture. Smoke patties of ground sausage, crumble into small pieces and substitute in place of smoked chicken. Smoked mushrooms are also a great addition to this recipe.

ALDER SMOKED SALMON SPREAD WITH JALAPEÑO CREAM CHEESE

Alder smoke gives salmon a delicious mellow flavor. When combined with jalapeño, chili powder, cilantro and cream cheese, the result is a spicy but smooth taste sensation. Enjoy it as an appetizer, tapas or as a delicious sandwich.

Ingredients:

4 alder wood chunks (use hickory as substitute)

1 bottle (750 ml) fruity sweet wine (Johannisberg Riesling or white Zinfandel)

2 8-oz skinless salmon fillets

$1/2$ cup cream cheese

2 pickled jalapeño peppers, minced with seeds and stems removed

$1/4$ cup chopped fresh cilantro

2 tablespoons fresh lemon juice

$1/2$ teaspoon pure chili powder

Salt to taste

Place wood chunks on charcoal or lava rocks, and pour wine into water pan. Place salmon in smoker basket (see page 18) and set on lower level grill. Smoke cook for approximately 45 minutes to 1 hour (electric/gas smoker) or 1 to $1^{1}/_{2}$ hours (charcoal smoker).

Remove salmon from smoker and place in mixing bowl. Mash smoked salmon into tiny flakes by using the back side of a fork or spoon. Add cream cheese, jalapeño, cilantro, lemon juice and chili powder. Blend well into a smooth mixture. Add salt to taste and blend again.

Cover mixture and refrigerate for at least 2 hours. Serve on toasted French bread or crackers as an appetizer or in a sandwich with lettuce and tomato. Serves 6.

ALDER SMOKED TUNA SPREAD WITH TABASCO CREAM CHEESE

For a spicy tuna spread, substitute 16 oz white albacore tuna packed in water in place of the salmon. Place large chunks of tightly packed tuna in smoker basket. Cold smoke (see page 23) for 30 to 45 minutes. Substitute 1 teaspoon of Tabasco sauce in place of jalapeño peppers.

MESQUITE SMOKED BEEF TENDERLOIN CHILI WITH DARK BEER

*T*his chili has a robust smoky flavor derived from the smoked tenderloin. Using dark beer as the steam marinade and as an ingredient in the chili adds another delicious dimension to this gourmet chili recipe. Serve as an entrée, as a sauce for enchiladas and tamales or as a topping for nachos.

Ingredients:

A 6-lb beef tenderloin, trimmed of fat

4 mesquite wood chunks (use pecan or oak as substitute)

6 cups dark beer for water pan

1 cup canola oil

1¹/₂ large onions, finely chopped

4 cloves garlic, minced

3 tablespoons pure chili powder

2 teaspoons ground cumin

1¹/₂ teaspoons minced parsley

3 teaspoons minced oregano

10 large ripe tomatoes, blanched, peeled and diced

5 tablespoons tomato paste

2 cups chicken stock, preferably homemade (if using canned broth, use only No MSG type)

1 cup dark beer for chili

Salt to taste

3 cups shredded Cheddar cheese for garnish

Slice raw tenderloin into 1¹/₂-inch thick slices. Use an ice pick or long pronged fork to poke holes throughout the tenderloin slices so aromatic smoke and steam marinade can easily penetrate the meat. Place wood chunks on charcoal or lava rocks, and pour beer into water pan. Place tenderloin slices in smoker basket (see page 18) and set on lower level grill. Smoke cook for 45 minutes to 1 hour (electric/gas smoker) or 1 to 1¹/₂ hours (charcoal smoker). The meat should be a medium rare doneness. The tenderloin will be cooked further with the chili mixture, so be careful not to overcook it in the smoker. Use a meat thermometer to test doneness.

Remove tenderloin from smoker. As soon as meat is cool enough to handle, chop smoked tenderloin into tiny pieces. Heat oil over medium heat in a large stew pan. Add smoked tenderloin pieces, onion and garlic, and sauté for about 10 minutes. Add all remaining ingredients except salt and cheese and bring to a full boil. Lower heat and simmer uncovered for 1¹/₂ hours until thickened, stirring frequently. Salt to taste. Serve in bowls and garnish liberally with cheese. Serves 10.

MESQUITE SMOKED VENISON TENDERLOIN CHILI WITH DARK BEER

For venison lovers, there is no better way to prepare venison than in chili. Follow the above recipe and substitute venison tenderloin in place of beef, and substitute Feta in place of Cheddar cheese.

OAK SMOKED RACK OF LAMB BASTED IN FRESH GARLIC AND MUSTARD

This recipe has its roots in the hill country of Texas where raising and cooking lamb is prevalent. I didn't realize how much I loved the flavor of lamb until I tasted it smoked. Smoked rack of lamb is one of the easiest and most delicious gourmet dishes I prepare. It's fabulous as an entrée and quite impressive as finger food at a party.

Ingredients:

A 12-bone rack of lamb, trimmed of fat

1 cup coarse ground prepared mustard (German style or Dijon is best)

10 large cloves garlic, halved

4 oak wood chunks (use hickory as substitute)

1 bottle (750ml) Cabernet Sauvignon or Merlot red wine for water pan

$^1/_2$ cup each honey and Dijon mustard for sauce

Coat rack of lamb with mustard. Using a small sharp knife, cut slits the length of the garlic cloves all over the top side of the lamb. Insert garlic clove halves into slits.

Place wood chunks on charcoal or lava rocks, and pour wine into water pan. Place lamb rack, top side up, in smoker basket (see page 18) and set on lower level grill. Smoke cook for approximately 1 to $1^1/_2$ hours (electric/gas smoker) or 2 to $2^1/_2$ hours (charcoal smoker) for medium rare to medium doneness. When sliced, the lamb chop should have a slightly pink center. Be careful not to overcook. Use a meat thermometer to test doneness.

Slice chops between bones and serve. For sauce, mix honey and mustard and serve a small portion on the side. Serves 6.

OAK SMOKED PORK CROWN RIB ROAST BASTED IN HONEY MUSTARD

For the best pork rib roast you've ever tasted, follow the above recipe, add 1 cup of honey to the mustard and coat the roast with this mixture. Pork should be cooked a little longer for a medium to medium well doneness; I always use a meat thermometer. This dish is good served with cornbread dressing.

HICKORY SMOKED TOMATO SOUP WITH SOUR CREAM AND BASIL

*O*nce you've tasted smoked tomato soup, you will never want to eat plain tomato soup again. The blending of smoke, tomatoes, basil and sour cream is a culinary delight you won't soon forget. This is the ultimate gourmet tomato soup, and it's so easy to prepare. Serve as a first course before the smoked tenderloin or smoked rack of lamb.

Ingredients:

3 hickory wood chunks

4 cups water for water pan

8 medium ripe tomatoes, halved

3 medium carrots, peeled

1 red bell pepper

½ cup chicken stock, preferably homemade (if using canned broth, use only No MSG type)

½ cup chopped fresh basil

2 cups half-and-half

½ cup sour cream

Salt to taste

Fresh basil leaves for garnish

Place wood chunks on charcoal or lava rocks, and pour water into water pan. Place tomato halves (cut side up), whole carrots and whole red bell pepper in smoker basket (see page 18) and set on lower level grill. Smoke cook for approximately 30 minutes (electric/gas smoker) or 40 minutes (charcoal smoker) until skins of tomatoes and pepper begin to blister and peel.

Remove vegetables from smoker. Remove stems, skin and seeds from tomatoes and pepper. Purée the smoked vegetables in a blender or food processor. In a sauce pan, heat chicken stock over medium heat and add smoked vegetable purée and basil. Bring to a boil, reduce heat and simmer for 5 minutes. Add half-and-half and sour cream and stir vigorously until smooth. Cook uncovered on low heat for about 20 to 30 minutes until thickened. You will need to add enough salt to bring flavor into balance.

Serve piping hot in soup bowls and garnish with small basil leaves. Good with French bread. Serves 6.

HICKORY SMOKED TOMATO SOUP WITH SOUR CREAM, CHILI AND CILANTRO

For a spicy Southwestern style smoked tomato soup, substitute fresh cilantro in place of the basil and add 1 tablespoon of pure chili powder. Serve with warm flour tortillas.

MAPLE SMOKED BABY BACK RIBS STEAMED IN BOURBON MARINADE

*S*moked ribs are a tried and true favorite. This recipe uses a sweet plum, honey and bourbon glaze to balance the smoky flavor. Bourbon in the water pan gently steams and marinates the ribs to tender perfection. If you're serving beans as a side dish, put the pot of beans in the smoker to let them take on a smoky flavor.

Ingredients:

1 cup honey

1 cup plum preserves

¹/₂ cup bourbon

1 teaspoon salt

8 lb baby back ribs in slabs

4 maple wood chunks (use hickory as substitute)

4 cups bourbon for water pan

Orange zest for garnish

In a sauce pan over medium heat mix honey, plum preserves, bourbon and salt. Simmer, stirring frequently, for about 20 minutes until bourbon is reduced and sauce thickens to a thick glaze. Saturate ribs with glaze.

Place wood chunks on charcoal or lava rocks, and pour bourbon into water pan. Place glazed ribs, meaty side up, in smoker basket or rib-rack holder (see page 19) and place on lower level grill. Smoke cook for approximately 45 minutes to 1 hour (electric/gas smoker) or 1 to 1¹/₂ hours (charcoal smoker). About 15 minutes before ribs are done, brush with additional glaze.

Garnish with orange zest. Serves 6.

MAPLE SMOKED BABY BACK RIBS STEAMED IN GRAND MARNIER

For a sweet orange flavor, substitute orange marmalade in place of plum preserves and Grand Marnier in place of bourbon.

If you're planning a party and need to cook several racks at a time, be sure to pick up a couple of rib-rack holders.

PECAN SMOKED GARLIC MEATBALLS WITH FETTUCCINI IN RED SAUCE

*L*ots of fresh garlic, Parmesan cheese and pecan smoke make these meatballs a special treat the whole family will love. They can be served with pasta and red sauce as they are in this recipe, as an appetizer or in a meatball sandwich.

Ingredients:

$\frac{1}{4}$ cup extra virgin olive oil

1 large onion, chopped

10 cloves garlic, minced

2 lb extra lean ground beef or veal

$\frac{3}{4}$ cup freshly grated Parmesan cheese

5 tablespoons tomato paste

5 tablespoons tomato catsup

1 cup Italian bread crumbs

3 large eggs, beaten

$\frac{1}{3}$ cup each finely chopped fresh basil, oregano and parsley

1 teaspoon freshly ground pepper

2 teaspoons salt

4 pecan wood chunks (use hickory as substitute)

$\frac{1}{2}$ cup garlic powder and 5 cups water for water pan

32 oz of your favorite red pasta sauce

$1\frac{1}{2}$ lb fettuccini, cooked al dente

1 cup freshly grated Parmesan cheese for garnish

Heat olive oil in a sauce pan over medium heat and cook onion for about 10 to 15 minutes until transparent, stirring frequently. Add garlic and cook until light golden brown, about 5 minutes. Set aside to cool. With wet hands to prevent sticking, blend ground meat, Parmesan, tomato paste, catsup, bread crumbs, eggs and spices in a large mixing bowl. Add cooled garlic and onion mixture and blend thoroughly. Roll meat mixture into balls the size of golf balls.

Place wood chunks on charcoal or lava rocks, and pour garlic powder and water mixture into water pan. Evenly distribute meatballs on one layer in smoker basket (see page18) and set on lower level grill. Smoke cook for approximately $1\frac{1}{2}$ to 2 hours (electric/gas smoker) or 2 to $2\frac{1}{2}$ hours (charcoal smoker).

Combine red sauce and smoked meatballs in a sauce pan and simmer over medium heat for about 10 minutes. Add cooked pasta and heat until piping hot, stirring frequently. Serve garnished with Parmesan cheese. Serves 6.

PECAN SMOKED GARLIC AND PARMESAN CHEESE MEATLOAF

For a deliciously different meatloaf, add 1 cup finely chopped celery to the meat mixture. Form into a loaf and place in smoker basket (see page 18). Smoke cook on lower level grill approximately 2 to $2\frac{1}{2}$ hours (electric/gas smoker) or 3 to 4 hours (charcoal smoker).

---

*S*moking the chicken and sun-dried tomatoes brings a whole new dimension to paella. If you like, add other smoked ingredients such as sausage, pork or beef. Seafood paellas should be made with saffron instead of cumin.

Ingredients:

3 walnut wood chunks (use hickory or alder as substitute)

1/4 cup ground cumin and 5 cups water for water pan

4 skinless boneless chicken breasts

12 sun-dried tomatoes packed in olive oil

1/4 cup extra virgin olive oil

Salt and freshly ground pepper to taste

4 cloves garlic, minced

1 medium onion, chopped

3 tablespoons pine nuts

2 cups white rice, preferably short grain

4 cups chicken stock, preferably homemade (if using canned broth, use No MSG type)

1/2 cup chopped fresh parsley

1 teaspoon ground cumin

1/4 cup green olives, pitted and sliced

Place wood chunks on charcoal or lava rocks, and pour cumin and water mixture into water pan. Place chicken breasts and sun-dried tomatoes in smoker basket (see page 18) and set on lower level grill. Smoke cook for about 20 minutes (electric/gas smoker) or 30 minutes (charcoal smoker). The chicken should be slightly undercooked as it will be sautéed in olive oil later. Remove chicken and tomatoes from smoker and slice chicken into 1/4-inch thick medallions.

Heat olive oil in a sauce pan over medium-high heat. Sprinkle smoked chicken medallions with salt and pepper and brown in hot oil, about 30 to 60 seconds on each side. Transfer browned smoked chicken to a plate. Add onion to oil, reduce heat to medium and sauté for about 10 minutes. Then add garlic, pine nuts and tomatoes and sauté for another 5 minutes. Add uncooked rice and sauté over low heat, stirring, for 3 to 4 minutes. Stir in heated chicken stock, parsley, ground cumin, green olives and chicken medallions. Reduce heat to low, cover and simmer for 30 to 40 minutes until rice is tender and liquid is absorbed. Serves 6.

ALDER SMOKED SALMON PAELLA WITH SUN-DRIED TOMATOES AND PINE NUTS

For a seafood paella, substitute 24 oz skinless salmon fillets in place of the chicken. Use alder wood instead of walnut and use a bottle of sweet, fruity Johannisberg Riesling or white Zinfandel wine in the water pan instead of cumin and water. Also, eliminate the ground cumin in the recipe and add 3/4 teaspoon crushed saffron threads in its place.

HICKORY SMOKED SAUSAGE AND BACON OMELET WITH CHEDDAR & JACK CHEESE

*T*he mellow flavor of eggs and cheese is a perfect balance for smoky sausage and bacon. This omelet is perfect for a Sunday brunch. Smoke a few extra strips of bacon and serve with the omelet.

Ingredients:

4 hickory wood chunks

5 cups beer for water pan

8 oz ground breakfast sausage

8 strips bacon

4 tablespoons extra virgin olive oil

$^1/_2$ cup chopped onion

$^1/_2$ cup chopped green bell pepper

1 cup chopped tomato

12 large fresh eggs

4 tablespoons butter

1$^1/_2$ cups shredded Cheddar cheese

1$^1/_2$ cups shredded Monterey Jack cheese

$^1/_2$ cup chopped fresh parsley

Place wood chunks on charcoal or lava rocks, and pour beer into water pan. Form four round sausage patties. Place sausage patties and bacon strips in smoker basket (see page 18) and set on lower level grill. Smoke cook for approximately 30 to 45 minutes (electric/gas smoker) or 45 minutes to 1 hour (charcoal smoker) until sausage and bacon are fully cooked. Remove smoked sausage and bacon from smoker and crumble into $^1/_4$-inch pieces. Cover and set aside.

Heat olive oil in sauté pan over medium heat. Sauté onion and pepper in olive oil, stirring frequently, until onion is light golden brown, about 10 to 15 minutes. Add tomato, bacon and sausage, cover and simmer on low heat for another 10 minutes, stirring occasionally. Remove from heat, keep covered and set aside for omelet filling.

Beat 3 eggs each in separate bowls for omelets and set aside. Melt 1 tablespoon butter in a 6- to 8-inch omelet pan to prepare each omelet individually. Just before eggs are fully cooked, add 4 tablespoons of warm omelet filling and a liberal amount of Cheddar and Monterey Jack cheese. Fold omelet over. Cook another 20 to 30 seconds over low heat and transfer to a warm plate. Garnish with another spoonful of filling, cheese and chopped parsley. Makes 4 omelets.

HICKORY SMOKED MUSHROOM AND ONION OMELET WITH GOUDA CHEESE

For a delicious mushroom and onion omelet, smoke cook 12 large mushrooms for 30 minutes on lower level grill using hickory wood and plain water in water pan. To prepare omelet filling, slice smoked mushrooms into small pieces and sauté with $^3/_4$ cup chopped onion in 4 tablespoons olive oil for 15 minutes. Prepare 3-egg omelets, add smoked mushroom-onion filling and plenty of shredded Gouda cheese.

PECAN SMOKED PORK TENDERLOIN ENCHILADAS WITH SMOKED RED PEPPER SAUCE

These spicy black bean and pork enchiladas are reminiscent of old Mexico. The serrano chilies and red chili powder add just the right amount of spice to the flavor of smoked pork and red peppers.

Ingredients:

4 pecan wood chunks
(use mesquite as substitute)

5 cups beer for water pan

Canola oil for softening tortillas

18 corn tortillas

6 cups shredded Monterey Jack cheese

Meat Filling:

A 4-lb pork tenderloin

¹/₄ cup extra virgin olive oil

2 cups chopped onions

2 cloves garlic, minced

2 cups cooked black beans, drained

2 tablespoons pure chili powder

¹/₂ cup chicken stock

Salt to taste

Sauce:

2 red bell peppers, halved

6 large ripe tomatoes, halved

2 cups chicken stock

5 cloves garlic, minced

2 cups chopped onion

4 serrano chilies, seeded and chopped

¹/₄ cup chopped fresh cilantro

Salt to taste

Place wood chunks on charcoal or lava rocks, and pour beer into water pan. Slice tenderloin into ¹/₄-inch thick slices. Place in smoker basket (see page 18) and set on lower level grill. Place red bell peppers and tomatoes (cut side up) in another smoker basket and set on upper level grill. Smoke cook for approximately 30 minutes (electric/gas smoker) or 40 minutes (charcoal smoker). The tenderloin should be medium rare as it will be cooked further with the filling mixture. Remove tenderloin and vegetables from smoker. Slice smoked tenderloin into bite-sized pieces, cover and set aside. Remove skin and seeds from smoked peppers and tomatoes.

To make sauce, purée (in a food processor or blender) smoked vegetables and all other sauce ingredients except cilantro and salt. In a sauce pan, cook the puréed mixture over medium-high heat for 10 to 15 minutes, stirring frequently. Just before removing sauce from heat, season with salt, add cilantro and set aside.

To make filling, sauté onion in olive oil for 10 minutes over medium heat. Add garlic and smoked tenderloin and sauté for another 5 minutes. Add all other filling ingredients except salt and cheese. Bring to a boil, reduce heat and simmer for 10 minutes. Season with salt, cover and set aside.

Heat ¹/₂ inch of canola oil in skillet over medium heat until barely smoking (350° F.). Soften tortillas by submerging them in oil (one at a time) for 5 seconds, and drain on paper towels. Spread 3 to 4 heaping tablespoons of filling mixture and 3 tablespoons of cheese down the center of each tortilla. Roll up tortillas and place them close together in a 3-to 4-inch deep baking dish, seam side down. Pour sauce mixture over enchiladas and top with remaining cheese. Cover and bake in preheated 350° F. oven for 15 minutes. Serves 6.

MESQUITE SMOKED SWORDFISH WITH SMOKED RED PEPPER AND BASIL CREAM SAUCE

*O*nce you taste this savory sauce flavored with smoked red pepper, Crème Fraiche and basil, you will want to try it with all types of fish, shellfish, beef, pork and pasta. For a Cajun style cream sauce, replace the basil with a half teaspoon of Tabasco.

Ingredients:

4 mesquite wood chunks

4 cups dry white wine for water pan

4 center-cut swordfish steaks, $1/2$-inch thick

2 medium red bell peppers, halved

3 medium ripe tomatoes, halved

2 tablespoons extra virgin olive oil

4 tablespoons chopped onion

2 cloves garlic, minced

2 tablespoons tomato paste

$1/4$ cup chopped fresh basil

$1/2$ cup Crème Fraiche or sour cream

Salt and freshly ground pepper

Place wood chunks on charcoal or lava rocks, and pour wine into water pan. Place swordfish in smoker basket (see page 18) and set on lower level grill. Place bell peppers and tomatoes (cut side up) in another smoker basket and set on upper level grill. Smoke cook swordfish and vegetables for 30 to 45 minutes (electric/gas smoker) or 45 minutes to 1 hour (charcoal smoker). Place smoked swordfish in a covered skillet to keep warm.

To make sauce, peel and seed smoked peppers and tomatoes, purée in a blender or food processor and set aside. In a sauce pan, heat olive oil over medium heat and sauté onion for 10 minutes. Add garlic and sauté for 5 minutes more. Add smoked pepper/tomato purée and tomato paste. Bring to a boil, stirring frequently. Reduce heat, add basil and Crème Fraiche or sour cream and stir until smooth. Season with salt and pepper.

To heat smoked swordfish, add a splash of water to the skillet, cover and steam for 2 minutes. Serve swordfish on warm plates and top with a generous portion of sauce. Serves 4.

ALDER SMOKED TERIYAKI SALMON WITH SESAME SEEDS

For an easy Oriental style smoked salmon, coat 4 skinless salmon fillets in a thick teriyaki glaze (Kikkoman Baste & Glaze is wonderful) and sprinkle with toasted sesame seeds. Smoke cook as directed above using alder wood chunks (or you may substitute hickory). Brush salmon with glaze again about 15 minutes before removing from smoker. Serve salmon on warm plates and garnish with more toasted sesame seeds.

*T*hese fun and easy smoked cheese snacks are delicious as an appetizer or a light meal. The trick is toasting the bread first, then cooking on the upper grill using low heat so the cheese doesn't melt too fast.

Ingredients:

1 large loaf Italian or French bread, 1-inch slices

¹/₂ cup extra virgin olive oil

3 hickory wood chunks

4 cups water for water pan

Italian Style:

3 ripe tomatoes, sliced

1 tablespoon chopped fresh basil

¹/₂ lb fresh mozzarella cheese, ¹/₄-inch slices

¹/₄ cup freshly grated Parmesan cheese

Mexican Style:

¹/₂ cup refried beans

4 pickled jalapeño peppers, sliced

1 tablespoon chopped fresh cilantro

¹/₂ lb Monterey Jack cheese, ¹/₄-inch slices

California Style:

6 cloves garlic, minced

3 avocados, sliced

1 sweet red onion, thinly sliced

¹/₂ lb Swiss cheese, ¹/₄-inch slices

Lightly toast bread slices. Brush top sides of toast liberally with olive oil. Evenly distribute toppings on toasted bread, building the ingredients in the order listed with cheese on top.

Place wood chunks on charcoal or lava rocks, and pour water into water pan. If using a charcoal smoker, use only about ¹/₄ pan of charcoal to keep cheese from melting too fast. Place cheese bread snacks in baking pan and set on upper level grill. Smoke cook until cheese is melted, checking frequently to avoid overcooking. If using an electric or gas smoker, I recommend turning the smoker off once the cheese snacks are inside (you can always turn the smoker back on for a few minutes if more cooking is necessary). Serve warm. These snacks can also be prepared in advance, refrigerated, and reheated in the oven. Serves 4.

HICKORY SMOKED MUSHROOM AND CHEESE PIZZA SNACKS

For pizza lovers, brush toasted bread slices with olive oil. Add your favorite pizza sauce, sliced mushrooms and mozzarella cheese. Smoke cook in baking pan as directed above until cheese is melted.

Smoke cooking imparts a delightful flavor to shellfish – so good, in fact, that I rarely prepare it any other way. In this recipe, the shrimp are cold smoked and then sautéed to seal in this mellow sweet flavor. The sautéed scallions and barbecue sauce combination makes for a zesty sauce that complements the pasta and smoked shrimp. This is also a great recipe for smoked crab, clams or calamari.

Ingredients:

3 oak wood chunks (use hickory as substitute)

20 fresh medium raw shrimp, peeled and deveined

6 tablespoons extra virgin olive oil

6 small green onions (scallions), chopped

3 cloves garlic, minced

$^1/_2$ cup thick barbecue sauce

$^1/_2$ teaspoon pure chili powder

$^1/_2$ cup dry white wine

$1^1/_2$ lb penne pasta, cooked al dente and drained

Salt and freshly ground pepper

1 cup freshly grated Parmesan cheese

2 tablespoons chopped fresh chives

Place wood chunks on charcoal or lava rocks; do not use liquid in water pan. Arrange shrimp in smoker basket (see page 18) and set on upper level grill. Cold smoke (see page 23) shrimp for 20 to 30 minutes.

In a sauce pan, heat olive oil over medium heat and sauté scallions and garlic for 5 minutes, stirring frequently. Add smoked shrimp and sauté for 2 to 3 minutes on each side until done. Remove shrimp, cover and set aside. Add heated barbecue sauce, chili powder and wine. Bring to a boil, stirring frequently. Add pasta, toss and heat until piping hot. Add smoked shrimp and heat 1 minute more. Season with salt and pepper. Serve in warm pasta bowls and garnish with Parmesan cheese and chives. Serves 4.

OAK SMOKED SEA SCALLOPS WITH LINGUINI IN GARLIC BUTTER SAUCE

For a delicious scallop and pasta dish, cold smoke 20 fresh sea scallops (washed, dried and coated with olive oil) for 20 to 30 minutes. Sauté 4 cloves minced garlic in 1 stick unsalted butter for 2 to 3 minutes. Add smoked scallops and cook two minutes on each side. Remove scallops, cover and set aside. Add linguini to sauce and toss until piping hot. Add smoked scallops and heat 1 minute more. Season with salt and pepper. Garnish with Parmesan cheese and chives.

GRAPEVINE AND ROSEMARY SMOKED VEGETABLE MEDLEY

Smoked vegetables are healthy and delicious as a side dish or a light meal. Almost any vegetable can be smoked, so experiment with your own favorites. Add smoked vegetables to soups, stews, rice dishes, bean dishes, casseroles, pastas, salads — any dish that uses vegetables — to perk up old recipes or create new ones.

Ingredients:

8 sticks dried grapevine (use hickory as substitute)
1 cup dried rosemary
5 cups water for water pan
2 ears corn, sliced in 2-inch sections
3 red bell peppers, seeded and sliced
4 medium scallions, whole
4 heads garlic, halved

4 zucchini squash, sliced
4 yellow squash, sliced
2 large sweet onions, sliced
4 jalapeño peppers, seeded and halved
6 large mushrooms, halved
6 new potatoes, quartered
1/2 cup extra virgin olive oil
Salt and freshly ground pepper

Place grapevine and rosemary on charcoal or lava rocks, and pour water into water pan. Brush vegetables with olive oil, place in smoker basket (see page 18) and set on lower level grill. Smoke cook for 30 to 45 minutes (electric/gas smoker) or 45 minutes to 1 hour (charcoal smoker). Some vegetables will require longer cooking times than others. The potatoes, bell peppers, corn and onions may be placed in the smoker about 15 minutes prior to adding the other vegetables. If further cooking is required, place vegetables in a preheated oven and roast to desired tenderness. Season with salt and pepper. Serves 6.

GRAPEVINE AND BASIL SMOKED EGGPLANT AND MUSHROOMS WITH ANGEL HAIR PASTA

Brush sliced eggplant and mushrooms with olive oil and smoke cook as directed above with grapevine and dried basil. Dice smoked vegetables. In a sauce pan over medium heat, sauté minced garlic in olive oil for 5 minutes. Add a splash of dry white wine and smoked vegetables, and sauté for another 5 minutes. Add al dente cooked angel hair pasta, toss and heat until piping hot. Season with salt and pepper. Garnish with freshly grated Parmesan cheese.

HICKORY SMOKED PEACH PIE WITH SOUR CREAM AND NUTMEG

The tart flavors of peaches and lemon juice are complemented by sour cream and just a hint of hickory smoke. This scrumptious pie is wonderful served cold as a fruit cream pie or served slightly warm as a traditional fruit pie. Cold or warm, indulge yourself and impress your friends with this new twist on an old favorite.

Ingredients:

2 hickory wood chunks

6 cups fresh ripe peaches (about 8 peaches), peeled and sliced

2 tablespoons lemon juice

3 tablespoons butter, softened to room temperature

3 tablespoons flour for dusting pan

Pie crust pastry for a two crust 9-inch pie (use your favorite recipe or ready-made pastry)

1 to 1^1/$_2$ cups sugar

^{1}/$_2$ cup sour cream or Crème Fraiche

^{1}/$_2$ cup flour, sifted

1 teaspoon grated nutmeg

Place wood chunks on charcoal or lava rocks; do not use liquid in water pan. Place 3 cups peaches in smoker basket (see page 18) and set on upper level grill. Cold smoke (see page 23) peaches for 10 minutes. Remove smoked peaches from smoker and combine with remaining unsmoked peaches and lemon juice. Cover and set aside.

Coat a 9-inch pie pan with 1^1/$_2$ tablespoons butter and lightly dust with flour. Line bottom of pie pan with pastry. Roll out pastry for top crust and cut into 1-inch wide strips for criss-cross pattern. Or, if you prefer, use a solid top crust with several slits to allow steam to escape.

In a mixing bowl blend sugar, sour cream or Crème Fraiche, flour and nutmeg. Gently fold in peaches and pour into pie pan. Place pastry strips close together in a decorative criss-cross pattern on top of peaches (or use a solid top crust with slits to allow steam to escape). Wet fingers with cold water and crimp edges of top and bottom crusts. Coat top crust with remaining softened butter.

Bake in a preheated 375° F. oven until peaches are bubbling and pastry is golden brown (about 1 hour to 1 hour 15 minutes). Set pie out to cool. Serve slightly warm or cold with whipped cream.

HICKORY SMOKED APPLE PIE WITH SOUR CREAM AND CINNAMON

For a delicious apple pie, use tart green apples (Granny Smith apples are my favorite) in place of the peaches and substitute ground cinnamon for nutmeg. Serve warm with ice cream or cold with whipped cream.

Index